D0354411

QUOTATIONS FROM
CHAIRMAN TRUMP

QUOTATIONS FROM CHAIRMAN TRUMP

Edited by Carol Pogash

RosettaBooks®
New York 2016

40000163141429

RosettaBooks editions are available to the trade through Ingram
distribution services, ipage.ingramcontent.com or (844) 749-4857. For
special orders, catalogues, events, image use, or other information,
please write to production@rosettabooks.com.

∞ This paper meets the requirements of ANSI/NISO Z39.48-1992
(Permanence of Paper), and is SFI certified.

Published 2016 by RosettaBooks

Cover and interior design and interior illustrations by Corina Lupp

ISBN (hardcover): 978-0-7953-4821-1

ISBN (EPUB): 978-0-7953-4815-0
ISBN (Kindle): 978-0-7953-4816-7

www.RosettaBooks.com

CONTENTS

★ TRUMP ON THE STUMP

★ ACKNOWLEDGEMENTS   180

★ ABOUT THE EDITOR   184

PREFACE

Donald Trump possesses a great sense of history and of himself. A model statesman, he speaks and tweets every thought, and more. With one exception, he does not suffer fools lightly. He's turned campaigning into a high-ratings blood sport. And he's transformed the once-stodgy rich man's Republican Party into a reality TV spectacle starring a multi-billionaire.

For all this, our nation owes Mr. Trump a debt of gratitude. It is because of his outsized impact on our body politic that this book was written. This little red book attempts to capture the great man's philosophy on governance, democracy, terrorism, and his hair.

With his winning message—"We'll have so much winning, you'll get bored with winning"—he joins a small cadre of great American orators. In time, the eloquence of his words will be woven into the fabric of our society and our T-shirts.

John F. Kennedy told the nation, "Ask not what your country can do for you; ask what you can do for your country." FDR assured a worried nation, "The only thing we have to fear is fear itself." Now we can add Donald Trump's line, "How stupid are the people of Iowa?"

Unlike some of our most revered presidents, Mr. Trump does not need a Ted Sorensen (JFK's speechwriter) or a Peggy Noonan (Ronald Reagan's speechwriter) to turn a phrase. He turns his own and, as he would point out, he does it better and for less money. He has an uncanny ability to speak his mind without a teleprompter or script, telling a losing nation, "I beat China all the time."

Mr. Trump, who believes he is always right, may be correct: he may become the forty-fifth president of the United States. Failing that, he could spend his later years constructing resorts and walls while representing the USA as a diplomat, possibly as ambassador to Mexico.

This is history on the fly, written for the scholars of the future who will analyze Trumpian doctrine and for the schoolchildren who will memorize Trump's pithiest quotes.

Here are the crème de la crème of Trump's lines, recorded as a public service and as a keepsake, to be passed down from one generation to the next.

—Carol Pogash
Trumplandia
USA!

THE
TALENTED
MR. TRUMP

★ ★ ★

*Everything I've done virtually
has been a tremendous success.*

SELF-REFLECTION

I'm Donald Trump. I wrote *The Art of the Deal*. I say not in a braggadocious way—I've made billions and billions of dollars dealing with people all over the world, and I want to put whatever that talent is to work for this country so we have great trade deals, we make our country rich again, we make it great again. We build our military, we take care of our vets, we get rid of Obamacare, and we have a great life altogether.

Trump's thirty-second chance to introduce himself to the nation. GOP presidential debate, September 16, 2015.

They say I'm the best-known businessman.

Interviewed by Sean Hannity on
Hannity, Fox News, June 17, 2015.

I don't have to brag. I don't have to, believe it
or not.

Announcing his run for president, Trump
Tower, New York City, June 16, 2015.

As a presidential candidate, I have instructed my long-time doctor to issue, within two weeks, a full medical report-it will show perfection.

Tweet, December 3, 2015.

"@HoustonWelder: Donald Trump is one of the sexiest men on this planet. Every woman dreams of a good man who tells it like it is." So true!

Retweet, July 16, 2015.

★

I DON'T KNOW HOW YOU WOULD DEFINE INSECURITY AS IT PERTAINS TO ME.

★

"Introducing Donald Trump, Diplomat,"
Maureen Dowd, The New York Times,
August 15, 2015.

THE GREAT LEADER

I'm a solid, stable person. I am a man of great achievement. I win, Maureen, I always win. Knock on wood. I win. It's what I do. I beat people. I win.

"Introducing Donald Trump, Diplomat," Maureen Dowd, The New York Times, *August 15, 2015.*

I understand business better than anybody that's ever run, in my opinion, for office.

Conservative Political Action Conference (CPAC), February 27, 2015.

Nobody knows more about the banking system than me, believe me.

Hannity, *November 17, 2015.*

Washington is totally broken and it's not going to get fixed unless we put the top person in that position.

Conservative Political Action Conference (CPAC), February 27, 2015.

I'm not a politician, thank goodness.

Conservative Political Action Conference (CPAC), February 27, 2015.

I actually think this election is going to be about competence. I'm a very competent person, okay? … Inequality is going to be a big issue, but competence is going to be the biggest issue. They want to see somebody that's super-competent and that's me.

"The Economist interviews Donald Trump," The Economist, *September 3, 2015.*

In New York, I'm king of zoning. I am going to build a wall, a Great Wall, and it will probably be named after me.

Speech at USS Wisconsin, *Norfolk, Virginia, October 30, 2015.*

Everything I've done virtually has been a tremendous success.

GOP presidential debate, September 16, 2015.

THE APPRENTICE

Well, I watch the shows. I mean, I really see a lot of great—you know, when you watch your show, and all of the other shows, and you have the generals, and you have certain people—

Responding to the question, "Who do you talk to for military advice right now?" Interviewed by Chuck Todd on Meet the Press, *NBC, August 16, 2015.*

I will know more about the problems of this world by the time I sit, and you look at what's going in this world right now by people that supposedly know, this world is a mess.

GOP presidential debate, September 16, 2015.

THE CHRISTIAN

Believe me, if I run and I win, I will be the greatest representative of the Christians they've had in a long time.

Interviewed by David Brody on The Brody File, *CBN, May 20, 2015.*

I think if I do something wrong, I think, I just try and make it right. I don't bring God into that picture. I don't.

Responding to Frank Luntz's question about whether he ever sought God's forgiveness. Q&A at the Family Leadership Summit in Ames, Iowa, July 18, 2015.

When I drink my little wine—which is about the only wine I drink—and have my little cracker, I guess that is a form of asking for forgiveness, and I do that as often as possible because I feel cleansed.

Q&A at the Family Leadership Summit in Ames, Iowa, July 18, 2015.

I'm strongly into the Bible; I'm strongly into
God and religion. I'm pro-life and different
things.

"The Economist interviews Donald Trump,"
The Economist, *September 3, 2015.*

What's my favorite book? The Bible!
The Bible.

At a rally in Mobile, Alabama, as tweeted by The
Washington Post*'s Robert Costa, August 23, 2015.*

Probably equal. The whole Bible is just incredible.

> *Responding to the question, "Are you an Old Testament guy or a New Testament guy?" Interviewed by Mark Halperin and John Heilemann on* With All Due Respect, *Bloomberg Television, August 26, 2015.*

I like the pope. ... He seems like a pretty good guy.

> *Interviewed by Chris Cuomo on* New Day, *CNN, August 20, 2015.*

I'd say ISIS wants to get [the pope].
You know that ISIS wants to go in and take
over the Vatican? You have heard that—
you know, that's a dream of theirs to go
into Italy....

*Responding to question asking what he
would say if the pope said capitalism causes
corruption and greed. Interviewed by Chris
Cuomo on* New Day, *CNN, August 20, 2015.*

Christians need support in our country
(and around the world), their religious liberty
is at stake! Obama has been horrible, I will
be great

Tweet, September 19, 2015.

I don't have to say it. ... I'm Presbyterian. I'm
Presbyterian. That's down the middle of the
road, folks. I mean, Seventh-day Adventist,
I just don't know about.

*Casting doubt on Dr. Ben Carson's religion. Rally in
Jacksonville, Florida, October 24, 2015.*

(See Dr. Ben Carson, page 64)

★

THE BIBLE
MEANS A LOT TO
ME, BUT I DON'T
WANT TO GET
INTO SPECIFICS.
...I DON'T WANT
TO GET INTO
VERSES.

★

INTERVIEWED BY MARK HALPERIN AND JOHN
HEILEMANN ON WITH ALL DUE RESPECT,
BLOOMBERG TELEVISION, AUGUST 26, 2015.

THE
ENVIRONMENTALIST

It's really cold outside, they are calling it a
major freeze, weeks ahead of normal. Man,
we could use a big fat dose of global warming!

Tweet, October 19, 2015.

I'm not a believer in man-made [climate
change]—look, this planet is so massive.
And when I hear Obama saying that climate
change is the number-one problem, it is just
madness.

Interviewed by Sean Hannity on
Hannity, Fox News, June 17, 2015.

If I am elected President I will immediately approve the Keystone XL pipeline. No impact on environment & lots of jobs for U.S.

Tweet, August 18, 2015.

So sad that Obama rejected Keystone Pipeline. Thousands of jobs, good for the environment, no downside!

Tweet, November 6, 2015.

THE DOCTOR

Autism has become an epidemic. Twenty-five years ago, thirty-five years ago, you look at the statistics, not even close. It has gotten totally out of control.

Answering a question on how he would handle childhood vaccinations when the Centers for Disease Control and Prevention and the National Institutes of Health say there is no connection between autism and vaccinations. GOP presidential debate, September 16, 2015.

Just the other day, two years old, two and a half years old, a child, a beautiful child went to have the vaccine, and came back, and a week later got a tremendous fever, got very, very sick, now is autistic.

Continuing to explain why the CDC and NIH are wrong and he's right. GOP presidential debate, September 16, 2015.

LIKE A REALLY SMART PERSON

I went to the Wharton School of Business…
I'm, like, a really smart person.

Speech in Phoenix, Arizona, July 11, 2015.

I'm the smart guy. I went to the Wharton
School of Finance. I was a really good student
and all that stuff, but then I built an empire.
I did *The Art of the Deal*. I did *The Apprentice*.
I've had an amazing life. I'm like the smart
person.

Interviewed by Don Lemon on CNN
Tonight, *CNN, August 7, 2015.*

I do a book called *The Art of the Deal*. It's probably the number-one-selling business book of all time. I go to the Wharton School of Finance. I was a good student in the hardest school there was to get into. ... And then they say, "Oh, he's not qualified," and they take some dope who becomes a senator, who doesn't have—who's nothing, and he's qualified to be on the stage, but Trump isn't qualified? Give me a break.

Responding to criticism that he doesn't belong on the presidential debate stage. Interviewed by Mark Halperin, Morning Joe, *MSNBC, June 18, 2015.*

I went to the Wharton School of Finance,
I was an excellent student, I'm a smart
person. I built a tremendous company.
I had a show called *The Apprentice* that NBC
desperately wanted me to do another season.
I do all this stuff. Do you think I'd make a
stupid statement like that? Who would make
a statement like that? Only a sick person
would even think about it.

> *Answering Jake Tapper's question: "You're saying*
> *that you did not mean to suggest that Megyn*
> *Kelly was having her period?" Trump earlier said*
> *Kelly had "blood coming out of her wherever."*
> State of the Union, *CNN, August 9, 2015.*

> *(See Megyn Kelly, page 44)*

I went to an Ivy League school. Like an intelligent person, I know when to speak.

Interviewed by Matt Lauer on The Today Show, *NBC, Atkinson, New Hampshire, October 26, 2015.*

Hey Bill, hey Bill, I went to an Ivy League school. I was a very good student. There's no problem with me going into details. I answer the way I want to answer.

Responding to criticism that he didn't provide details during the third GOP presidential debate. Interviewed by Bill O'Reilly on The O'Reilly Factor, *Fox News, October 29, 2015.*

PHILOSOPHER KING

When somebody challenges you unfairly,
fight back—be brutal, be tough—don't take it.
It is always important to WIN!

Tweet, June 27, 2015.

I think everyone's a threat to me.

*Talking about his competitors in the presidential
race. Interviewed by Chuck Todd,* Meet
the Press, *NBC, November 8, 2015.*

To be a winner you have to think like a winner.

Conservative Political Action Conference (CPAC), February 27, 2015.

Everybody that's hit me so far has gone down. They've gone down big league.

Speech in Sioux City, Iowa, October 27, 2015.

I'm too trusting, and when they let me down, if they let me down, I never forgive.

Responding to a question about his greatest weakness. GOP presidential debate, October 28, 2015.

If they do, I come after them times ten. That's the way the game is played.

Responding to Sean Hannity's question about how Trump will react to attack ads from fellow Republicans. Interviewed by Sean Hannity on Hannity, Fox News, November 9, 2015.

★

WHILE IN POLITICS IT IS OFTEN SMART TO SEND OUT FALSE MESSAGES...

★

TWEET, NOVEMBER 1, 2015.

SHOOTING STARS

★ ★ ★

I have a Gucci store that's worth more money than Romney.

FORMER GOVERNOR MITT ROMNEY

I'm the most successful person ever to run for president. I mean, off the record, Ross Perot isn't successful like me. Romney was— I have a Gucci store that's worth more money than Romney.

"I Won't Do Straw Poll if Everyone Backs Out," Josh Hafner, Des Moines Register, *June 1, 2015.*

AMBASSADOR CAROLINE KENNEDY

You know who's our primary representative [in Japan] now? Caroline Kennedy. You know how she got the job? She went to the White House, she said, "I'd love to have a job. I have nothing to do." They said, "How would you like to be the ambassador to Japan?" She goes, "Really?" And [Prime Minister Shinzo] Abe, who's a killer—he's great, he's already knocking the hell out of the yen—and he's wining and dining her. I watch him all the time wining and dining. Just doing a number on her.

Speech in Phoenix, Arizona, July 11, 2015.

ARIZONA SENATOR
JOHN MCCAIN

@SenJohnMcCain should be defeated in
the primaries. Graduated last in his class at
Annapolis—dummy!

*Tweeted response to Senator McCain saying
Trump's anti-immigration speech at a rally
in Phoenix, Arizona, "fired up the crazies," as
quoted in* The New Yorker, *July 16, 2015.*

He's a war hero because he was captured.
I like people that weren't captured, okay,
I hate to tell you.

*Senator McCain was shot down over North
Vietnam in 1967, fracturing his arms and legs.
Despite being tortured, he refused to be released
before his fellow American captives joined him.
He was set free in 1973. Q&A at the Family
Leadership Summit in Ames, Iowa, July 18, 2015.*

I supported him, I supported him for
president. I raised a million dollars for him,
that's a lot of money. I supported him.
He lost, he let us down, but, you know, he
lost. So, I've never liked him as much after
that, because I don't like losers.

*Q&A at the Family Leadership Summit
in Ames, Iowa, July 18, 2015.*

He's all talk and he's no action.

*Q&A at the Family Leadership Summit
in Ames, Iowa, July 18, 2015.*

The Veterans Administration is in shambles
and our veterans are suffering greatly.
John McCain has done nothing to help them
but talk.

Tweet, July 19, 2015.

People that fought hard and weren't captured and went through a lot, they get no credit. Nobody even talks about them. They're like forgotten. And I think that's a shame, if you want to know the truth.

Refusing to apologize for his comments about Senator McCain. Interviewed by Martha Raddatz, This Week, ABC News, June 19, 2015.

FORMER PRESIDENT
GEORGE W. BUSH

When you talk about George Bush, I mean—
say what you want —the World Trade Center
came down during his time.

Interviewed by Stephanie Ruhle on Bloomberg
GO, *Bloomberg Television, October 16, 2015.*

He was president, okay?

Interviewed by Stephanie Ruhle on Bloomberg
GO, *Bloomberg Television, October 16, 2015.*

FORMER PRESIDENT
BILL CLINTON

Had he not met Monica [Lewinsky], had he not met Paula [Jones], had he not met various and sundry semi-beautiful women, he would have had a much better deal going.

Interviewed by Mark Halperin,
Morning Joe, *MSNBC, June 18, 2015.*

MEGYN KELLY

She gets out and she starts asking me all sorts of ridiculous questions, and you know, you can see there was blood coming out of her eyes, blood coming out of her wherever.

> *Megyn Kelly is a Fox News anchor who during the first GOP debate asked Trump about remarks he has made calling women "fat pigs" and "dogs." Interviewed by Don Lemon on* CNN Tonight, *CNN, August 7, 2015.*

Certainly, I don't have a lot of respect for Megyn Kelly. She's a lightweight....

> *Interviewed by Don Lemon on* CNN Tonight, *CNN, August 7, 2015.*

I liked The Kelly File much better without @megynkelly. Perhaps she could take another eleven day unscheduled vacation!

Tweet, August 24, 2015.

ALL IN THE FAMILY

I wish good luck to all of the Republican
candidates that traveled to California to
beg for money etc. from the Koch Brothers.
Puppets?

Tweet, August 2, 2015.

(See following pages on GOP candidates)

KIDDIE TABLE

Governor Pataki, who, by the way, was a
failed governor in New York, a very seriously
failed—he wouldn't be elected dog catcher
right now.

GOP presidential debate, September 16, 2015.

Rick Perry failed at the border. Now he is
critical of me. He needs a new pair of glasses
to see the crimes committed by illegal
immigrants.

Tweet, July 5, 2015.

Oh wow, lightweight Governor @BobbyJindal, who is registered at less than 1 percent in the polls, just mocked my hair. So original!

Tweet, September 11, 2015.

There aren't a lot of people that would do that. He had a perfect opportunity to talk about himself, and he didn't do that, so he's a special guy.

Comment after Mike Huckabee didn't take the bait of moderators to comment on Trump's morals. Quoted by Jenna Johnson and Robert Costa for The Washington Post, *at a rally in Sparks, Nevada, October 29, 2015.*

OHIO GOVERNOR
JOHN KASICH

I built unbelievable companies worth billions and billions of dollars. I don't have to hear from this man. Believe me. I don't have to hear from him.

Responding to Gov. Kasich saying, "We can't ship eleven million people out of this country." GOP presidential debate, November 10, 2015.

CARLY FIORINA

Look at that face. Would anyone vote for that? Can you imagine that, the face of our next president?

> *"Trump Seriously: On the Trail With*
> *the GOP's Tough Guy," Paul Solotaroff,*
> Rolling Stone, *September 9, 2015.*

I think she's got a beautiful face, and I think she's a beautiful woman.

> *Backtracking at a GOP presidential*
> *debate, September 16, 2015.*

I just realized that if you listen to Carly Fiorina for more than ten minutes straight, you develop a massive headache. She has zero chance!

Tweet, August 9, 2015.

Carly whatever-the-hell-her-name-is…

Speech in Fort Dodge, Iowa, November 12, 2015.

KENTUCKY SENATOR RAND PAUL

A really nice guy. I mean, I've gotten to know him. I do like him a lot… I disagree with some of his policies, but that's okay.

Interviewed by Sean Hannity on
Hannity, Fox News, June 17, 2015.

He's very weak on the military. He's very weak on defense. And I think that's probably hurt him very badly. I think he's a nice guy.

Three days earlier, on July 30, 2015, Senator
Paul had attributed Trump's rise in the
polls to a "temporary loss of sanity." Trump
interviewed by Jonathan Karl on This
Week, ABC News, August 2, 2015.

Rand Paul shouldn't even be on this stage. He's number eleven, he's got 1 percent in the polls, and how he got up here, there's far too many people anyway.

> *On September 15, Rand Paul said when voters grasp who Trump is they will "run away with their hair on fire." GOP presidential debate, September 16, 2015.*

Truly weird Senator Rand Paul of Kentucky reminds me of a spoiled brat without a properly functioning brain. He was terrible at DEBATE!

> *Tweet, August 10, 2015.*

I truly understood the appeal of Ron Paul, but his son, @RandPaul, didn't get the right gene.

Tweet, September 12, 2015.

I never attacked him on his look, and believe me, there's plenty of subject matter right there.

> *Responding to Senator Paul's statement during the debate, "There's a sophomoric quality about Mr. Trump... his visceral response to attack people on their appearance, short, tall, fat, ugly." GOP presidential debate, September 16, 2015.*

Prediction: Rand Paul has been driven out of the race by my statements about him—he will announce soon. 1%!

> *As of December 7, 2015, Senator Paul was still in the race. Tweet, September 29, 2015.*

JEB!

The last thing we need is another Bush.

*Speech at Iowa Freedom Summit, Des
Moines, Iowa, January 24, 2015.*

Bush has no money. He's meeting today with
mommy and daddy and they're working on
their campaign.

Rally in Jacksonville, Florida, October 24, 2015.

Jeb Bush never uses his last name on advertising, signage, materials etc. Is he ashamed of the name BUSH?... Go Jeb!

Tweet, August 24, 2015.

Having trouble sleeping at night? Too much energy? Need some low energy? ... Jeb, for all your sleeping needs.

Instagram, September 8, 2015.

Okay, more energy tonight. I like that.

Reacting to Bush during a GOP presidential debate, September 16, 2015.

No @JebBush, you're pathetic for saying
nothing happened during your brother's term
when the World Trade Center was attacked
and came down.

Tweet, October 16, 2015.

@realDonaldTrump #JebBush has to like the Mexican Illegals because of his wife.

Retweeted and then deleted, July 4, 2015.

I think he's probably a nice guy.

Interviewed by Sean Hannity on Hannity, Fox News, June 17, 2015.

FLORIDA SENATOR
MARCO RUBIO

I don't understand why he's doing as well as he's doing, which isn't that well, frankly.

Interviewed by Sean Hannity on Hannity,
Fox News, November 3, 2015.

Marco Rubio is a total lightweight who I wouldn't hire to run one of my smaller companies...

Tweet, November 9, 2015.

[Rubio is] weak like a baby on immigration.

Speech in Fort Dodge, Iowa, November 12, 2015.

Marco Rubio couldn't even respond properly to President Obama's State of the Union Speech without pouring sweat & chugging water. He choked!

Tweet, November 9, 2015.

Since you're always sweating, we thought you could use some water. Enjoy!

Note sent to Rubio along with a case of Trump Ice Natural Spring Water, October 5, 2015.

Rubio an orator/liar like Obama but totally unqualified.

Tweet, October 30, 2015.

I see Marco Rubio just landed another billionaire to give big money to his Superpac, which are total scams. Marco must address him as "SIR"!

Tweet, October 31, 2015.

I think he's a lightweight. I hope I'm wrong about that.

Interviewed by Mark Halperin and John Heilemann on With All Due Respect, Bloomberg Television, November 2, 2015.

★

HE'S GOT NO MONEY, ZERO... HE'S GOT NOTHING.

★

Speech at South Carolina African American
Chamber of Commerce, North Charleston,
South Carolina, September 23, 2015.

DR. BEN CARSON

Well, I have a lot of respect for Ben Carson and I like him a lot. And we have had a very good relationship.

> *Trump in his short-lived bromance with the retired neurosurgeon, before Trump considered Dr. Carson a threat. Interviewed by Greta Van Susteren on* On the Record With Greta Van Susteren, *Fox News, September 21, 2015.*

We have a breaking story: Donald Trump has fallen to second place behind Ben Carson. We informed Ben, but he was sleeping.

> *Polls were showing Dr. Carson tied with Trump or ahead of him. "Bush Cuts Costs, Carson Eclipses Trump in Iowa and G.O.P. Frets," Patrick Healy and Trip Gabriel,* The New York Times, *October 24, 2015.*

We don't need somebody that doesn't make
a deal. He's never employed anybody, maybe
a nurse.

Interviewed by Sean Hannity on
Hannity, November 3, 2015.

Such bad reporting: A puff piece on Ben
Carson in the @nytimes states that Carson
"is trying to solidify his lead." But I am #1,
easily! Sad

Tweet, November 6, 2015.

I never tried to hit my mother in any way,
shape or form.

Interviewed by George Stephanopoulos on
This Week, ABC News, November 8, 2015.

He said he has a pathological disease in the book. When you have pathological disease, that's a very serious problem because that's not something that's cured.

> *Dr. Carson wrote that as a boy he had a pathological temper, attacking his mother and a friend. He wrote that he then went into his bathroom and prayed for three hours, and never had a problem with temper again. Interviewed by George Stephanopoulos on* This Week, *ABC News, November 8, 2015.*

I'm not looking to see anything bad happen to him.

> *Interviewed by Major Garrett,* Face the Nation, *CBS, November 8, 2015.*

Anybody have a knife and want to try it on me?

In a rambling ninety-five-minute speech,
Trump challenged the veracity of Dr. Carson's story
about stabbing a friend. Trump claimed it was
impossible for a belt buckle to stop the point of a knife.
Speech in Fort Dodge, Iowa, November 12, 2015.

If you're a child molester—a sick puppy—
you're a child molester, there's no cure for
that. … If you're a child molester, there's
no cure. They can't stop you. Pathological?
There's no cure.

Speech in Fort Dodge, Iowa, November 12, 2015.

He goes into the bathroom for a couple hours,
and comes out, and now he's religious. And
the people of Iowa believe him. Give me a
break.

Speech in Fort Dodge, Iowa, November 12, 2015.

★

*HOW STUPID
ARE THE PEOPLE
OF IOWA? HOW
STUPID ARE THE
PEOPLE OF THE
COUNTRY TO
BELIEVE THIS
CRAP?*

★

SPEECH IN FORT DODGE, IOWA, NOVEMBER 12, 2015.

TEXAS SENATOR
TED CRUZ

Well, I like him. He's been very strong
towards me. He's backed everything I've said.

> *Trump discussing potential vice presidential pick.*
> Laura Ingraham Show, *November 17, 2015.*

If he catches on, I guess we'll have to go to war.

> *CNBC's* Squawk Box, *November 16, 2015.*

FORMER SECRETARY OF STATE HILLARY CLINTON

Hillary is running for a lot of reasons. One of them is because she wants to stay out of jail.

Speech in Springfield, Illinois, November 9, 2015.

She was the worst secretary of state in the history of our nation.

Trump's statement came a day after Hillary Clinton said she was "very disappointed" in his remarks on immigration. Interviewed by Katy Tur on NBC Nightly News, NBC News, July 8, 2015.

I sort of laugh when I hear her talking about income inequality and she's taking in all of this money. And I know where they live and I know, you know, they live phenomenally and the money pours in.

Interviewed by Sean Hannity on Hannity, *Fox News, June 17, 2015.*

One person said she's a woman. That was the best answer.

Responding to Sean Hannity's question, "Can you name one thing—one specific thing that she's accomplished all these years she's been in the public eye that have made people's lives better?" Interviewed by Sean Hannity on Hannity, *Fox News, June 17, 2015.*

I said, "Be at my wedding," and she came to my wedding. You know why, she didn't have a choice because I gave. I gave to a foundation that, frankly, that foundation was supposed to do good. I didn't know her money would be used on private jets going all over the world. It was.

GOP presidential debate, August 6, 2015.

Huma Abedin, the top aide to Hillary Clinton and the wife of perv sleazebag Anthony Wiener, was a major security risk as a collector of info

Tweet, August 31, 2015.

Hillary said such nasty things about me, read directly off her teleprompter... but there was no emotion, no truth. Just can't read speeches!

Tweet, September 5, 2015.

Hillary Clinton is weak on illegal immigration, among many other things. She is strong on corruption—corruption is what she's best at!

Tweet, November 22, 2015.

Well, she has a new hairdo, did you notice
that today?

*Answering a question about Hillary Clinton's appeal
to voters. Interviewed by Mark Levin on* The Mark
Levin Show, *Cumulus Media, November 11, 2015.*

VERMONT SENATOR BERNIE SANDERS

I call him a socialist-slash-communist because that's what he is.

Rally in Richmond, Virginia, October 14, 2015.

Maniac.

Describing how Hillary Clinton is being pushed to the left by Bernie Sanders, whom he calls "this maniac." Rally in Richmond, Virginia, October 14, 2015.

(See Hillary Clinton, page 71)

He's gonna tax you people at 90 percent; he's gonna take everything.

Rally in Richmond, Virginia, October 14, 2015.

I would never give up my microphone. I thought that was disgusting. That showed such weakness, the way he was taken away by two young women—the microphone; they just took the whole place over.... That will never happen with me. I don't know if I'll do the fighting myself or if other people will, but that was a disgrace. I felt badly for him. But it showed that he's weak.

On August 8, 2015, Black Lives Matter protesters grabbed Sanders's microphone, preventing him from giving a speech in Seattle, Washington. Televised press conference in Birch Run, Michigan, August 11, 2015.

PRESIDENT
BARACK OBAMA

[Race relations are] almost as bad as they have ever been in the history of the country.

Describing race relations under President Obama. "The Economist interviews Donald Trump," The Economist, *September 3, 2015.*

I'm not a sitting senator, I'm not a sitting
anything else, I'm a good businessman—
but Trump comes along and I said, "Birth
certificate." He gave a birth certificate...
I certainly question it—but Hillary Clinton
wanted it, McCain wanted it, and I wanted it.
He didn't do it for them, he did it for me.

*There appears to be no record of Hillary Clinton
or John McCain requesting that Obama show
his birth certificate. Conservative Political
Action Conference, (CPAC), February 27, 2015.*

I don't talk about it anymore.

*Refusing to tell Stephen Colbert if he believes
President Obama was born in the United States.
Interviewed by Stephen Colbert on* The Late Show
with Stephen Colbert, *CBS, September 23, 2015.*

Our great African American President hasn't exactly had a positive impact on the thugs who are so happily and openly destroying Baltimore!

Tweet, April 28, 2015.

I would say he's incompetent but I don't want to do that because that's not nice.

GOP presidential debate, August 6, 2015.

I think he's a threat to this country. I mean he must have some kind of thing going because you know, when you see that he won't even call them by their name… It's radical Islamic terrorism and he won't even acknowledge it—it's like they're coming out of Denmark or something.

WRKO radio, Boston, Massachusetts,
November 18, 2015.

TRUMP ON
THE STUMP

★ ★ ★

I love the Muslims.
I think they're great people.

GIVE ME YOUR
TIRED, YOUR POOR

They're coming in now by the thousands and it's going to only get worse.

*Conservative Political Action Conference
(CPAC), February 27, 2015.*

When Mexico sends its people, they're not sending their best. They're not sending you. They're not sending you. They're sending people that have lots of problems, and they're bringing those problems with us. They're bringing drugs. They're bringing crime. They're rapists. And some, I assume, are good people.

Announcing his run for president, Trump Tower, New York City, June 16, 2015.

I love the Mexican people, but Mexico is not our friend. They're killing us at the border and they're killing us on jobs and trade. FIGHT!

Tweet, June 30, 2015.

Our Southern border is unsecure. I am the only one that can fix it, nobody else has the guts to even talk about it.

Tweet, July 3, 2015.

Miss Universe, Paulina Vega, criticized me
for telling the truth about illegal immigration,
but then said she would keep the crown-
Hypocrite

Tweet, July 5, 2015.

I'll get Mexico to pay for [the wall] one way or the other.

Interviewed by Chuck Todd on Meet the Press, *NBC, November 8, 2015.*

For those that don't think a wall (fence) works, why don't they suggest taking down the fence around the White House? Foolish people!

Tweet, August 31, 2015.

★

THE WALL WILL GO UP AND MEXICO WILL START BEHAVING.

★

INTERVIEWED BY BILL O'REILLY ON THE O'REILLY
FACTOR, FOX NEWS, JUNE 16, 2015.

@JeremyHL: RT @FoxNews: @realDonaldTrump: I have thousands of Hispanics working for me & they like me very much.

Tweet, October 14, 2015.

MSM are LYING to you about Hispanics hating Trump.

Retweet, November 5, 2015.

I don't have a racist bone in my body.

Interviewed on Entertainment Tonight, *July 1, 2015.*

CHERISHING WOMEN

Megyn Kelly: Mr. Trump, one of the things people love about you is you speak your mind and you don't use a politician's filter. However, that is not without its downsides, in particular, when it comes to women. You've called women you don't like 'fat pigs,' 'dogs,' 'slobs,' and 'disgusting animals.'

Trump: Only Rosie O'Donnell.

Kelly: For the record, it was well beyond Rosie O'Donnell.

Trump: Yes, I'm sure it was.

> *GOP presidential debate, August 6, 2015.*

If Hillary Clinton can't satisfy her husband what makes her think she can satisfy America? @realDonaldTrump #2016president

Retweet, April 16, 2015 (later deleted).

I think the big problem this country has is being politically correct.

Responding to Megyn Kelly's query about whether someone who tweets disparaging remarks about women's looks and tells a TV contestant it would be a pretty picture to see her on her knees has the temperament to be president. GOP presidential debate, August 6, 2015.

And frankly, what I say, and oftentimes it's fun, it's kidding. We have a good time.

Defending his derogatory remarks about women.
GOP presidential debate, August 6, 2015.

I will be phenomenal to the women. I want to help women.

Interviewed on Face the Nation,
CBS, August 9, 2015.

I've always been good to women and there
will be nobody better to women as a president,
because I'll take care—when I talk about
health issues, I will take care of women like
nobody else can. I will be so good to women.
I cherish women. I will be so good to women.
I will work hard to protect women.

Interviewed by Chris Cuomo on
New Day, *CNN, August 11, 2015.*

I find women to be amazing.

"Introducing Donald Trump, Diplomat,"
Maureen Dowd, The New York
Times, *August 15, 2015.*

Heidi Klum. Sadly, she's no longer a 10.

Heidi Klum is a 42-year-old German model,
businesswoman, and TV producer who has
appeared on the cover of Sports Illustrated.
"Introducing Donald Trump, Diplomat,"
Maureen Dowd, The New York
Times, *August 15, 2015.*

I respect women more than I respect men.
I have great respect, admiration. Hillary
Clinton said you shouldn't cherish women.
I do cherish women. I love women. My mother
was like the greatest woman I ever met. And
Hillary, who's become very shrill. You know
the word shrill? Shrill...

Speech at South Carolina African American
Chamber of Commerce, North Charleston,
South Carolina, September 23, 2015.

There's nobody that's better to women.

Interviewed by Matt Lauer on The Today Show,
NBC, Atkinson, New Hampshire, October 26, 2015.

My wife and Ivanka, women respect her so much, she said, "Dad, you respect and love women so much but people don't really understand how you feel."

Interviewed by Matt Lauer on The Today Show, *NBC, Atkinson, New Hampshire, October 26, 2015.*

MR. POPULARITY

Do we love these polls? Somebody said, "You love polls." I said that's only because I've been winning every single one of them. Right? Right? Every single poll...

Rally in Burlington, Iowa, October 21, 2015. "Bush Cuts Costs, Carson Eclipses Trump in Iowa and G.O.P. Frets," Patrick Healy and Trip Gabriel, The New York Times, *October 24, 2015.*

I think a lot of things are going to come out that are not so great for the opponents.

Discussing his campaign in Iowa, following news that polls put him in second place. Interviewed by Willie Geist on Morning Joe, *MSNBC, October 27, 2015.*

I'm a believer in polls. I only like them because I've been number one for one hundred days now, which is pretty good. How often do you see polls are wrong? Not too often.

"Donald Trump: On raising rates, running mates and Biden's decision," Susan Page, USA Today, October 22, 2015.

I honestly think those polls are wrong.

Responding after two polls found him trailing Dr. Ben Carson in Iowa. "Bush Cuts Costs, Carson Eclipses Trump in Iowa and G.O.P. Frets," Patrick Healy and Trip Gabriel, The New York Times, October 24, 2015.

Second is terrible to me.

Discussing his drop to second place in Iowa, at a speech in Sioux City, Iowa. Morning Joe, MSNBC, October 27, 2015.

THE AFRICAN
AMERICAN VOTE

As somebody said who's very much into this stuff, if you get 25 percent of the African American vote, the election's over. You win.

> *Citing a poll that predicted he would receive 25 percent of the African American vote in the general election. Speech at South Carolina African American Chamber of Commerce, North Charleston, South Carolina, September 23, 2015.*

I have a great relationship with African Americans, as you possibly have heard. I just have great respect for them. And they like me.

Interviewed by Anderson Cooper on Anderson Cooper 360, *CNN, July 22, 2015.*

THE MUSLIMS

I have friends that are Muslim. They're great people, amazing people. And most Muslims—like most everything—I mean, these are fabulous people. But we certainly do have a problem.

Interviewed by Jake Tapper on State of the Union, *CNN, September 20, 2015.*

I love the Muslims. I think they're great people.

Speech in Urbandale, Iowa, September 19, 2015.

I mean, it wasn't people from Sweden that blew up the World Trade Center, Jake.

Interviewed by Jake Tapper on State of the Union, *CNN, September 20, 2015.*

I would do that, absolutely. I think it's great.

Declaring he would be willing to close some US mosques to fight terrorism. Interviewed by Stuart Varney on Varney & Co., *Fox Business Network, October 20, 2015.*

You don't have to put on makeup. Wouldn't that be easier? I tell ya, if I was a woman... [Trump pretends he's putting on a burqa with the wave of his hand] "I'm ready darling, let's go."

"Donald Trump defends the burqa—in the most sexist way possible: 'You don't have to put on make-up,'" Sophia Tesfaye, Salon.com, October 26, 2015.

No, not at all.

Responding to a question from George Stephanopoulos: "Are you unequivocally now ruling out a database on all Muslims?" This Week, November 22, 2015.

Donald J. Trump is calling for a total and complete shutdown of Muslims entering the United States until our country's representatives can figure out what is going on.

Press release issued by Trump, December 7, 2015.

DOPES & CLOWNS

This political media, they are the worst. They are very dishonest, many of them.

> *Iowa Faith & Freedom Coalition Presidential Forum, Des Moines, Iowa, September 19, 2015.*

Go back to Univision.

> *Responding to well-known Hispanic journalist Jorge Ramos, who, while attending a Trump press conference, questioned Trump's plan to deport eleven million immigrants. Ramos was removed from the press conference and later allowed to return. Dubuque, Iowa, August 25, 2015.*

The liberal clown @ariannahuff told
her minions at the money losing
@HuffingtonPost to cover me as
enterainment. I am #1 in Huff Post Poll.

Tweet, July 18, 2015.

All I know is I have a very big group of
support, and I think one of the reasons is the
people don't trust you, and the people don't
trust the media. And I understand why.

Interviewed by Anderson Cooper on Anderson
Cooper 360, *CNN, July 22, 2015.*

I hear that sleepy eyes @chucktodd will
be fired like a dog from ratings starved Meet
The Press? I can't imagine what is taking
so long!

Tweet, July 12, 2015.

@MarthaRaddatz was so unprofessional and
biased when discussing me on This Week.
@GStephanopoulos should not allow this
conduct!

Tweet, June 21, 2015.

★

THE SCUM BACK THERE.

★

TRUMP'S DESCRIPTION OF THE MEDIA AT HIS RALLY
AFTER GOP PRESIDENTIAL DEBATE, SPARKS,
NEVADA, OCTOBER 29, 2015.

Little Barry Diller, who lost a fortune on Newsweek and Daily Beast, only writes badly about me. He is a sad and pathetic figure. Lives lie!

> *On October 6, Barry Diller said if Trump becomes president he'll leave the country "or join the resistance." Tweet, October 10, 2015.*

I was so happy when I heard that @Politico, one of the most dishonest political outlets, is losing a fortune. Pure scum!

> *Tweet, October 8, 2015.*

Failing host @glennbeck, a mental basketcase, loves SUPERPACS—in other words, he wants your politicians totally controlled by lobbyists!

> *Tweet, October 29, 2015.*

The @WSJ Wall Street Journal loves to write badly about me. They better be careful or I will unleash big time on them. Look forward to it!

Tweet, October 31, 2015.

Wow, great news! I hear @EWErickson of Red State was fired like a dog. If you read his tweets, you'll understand why. Just doesn't have IT!

After Trump made his disparaging remarks about Megyn Kelly, Erick Erickson disinvited Trump to one of his gatherings. Tweet, October 8, 2015.

I love *The New York Times*… I'm always on the front page of *The New York Times*. We're going to set a record for that, too.

Rally in Greenville, South Carolina, August 27, 2015.

So, since the people at the @nytimes have made all bad decisions over the last decade, why do people care what they write. Incompetent!

One of a series of anti-NYT tweets Trump posted a day after a New York Times *editorial referred to his "racist lies" and likened his demagoguery to that of Joseph McCarthy and George Wallace. Tweet, November 25, 2015.*

I think they should give me an apology before they go out of business.

Trump requesting an apology from The New York Times *after the paper criticized him for publicly ridiculing the disability of a* New York Times *reporter. Sarasota, Florida, November 28, 2015.*

FOX & FOES

@FoxNews you should be ashamed of yourself. I got you the highest debate ratings in your history & you say nothing but bad...

Tweet, August 7, 2015.

@KarlRove wasted $400 million + and didn't win one race—a total loser. @FoxNews

On July 8, Karl Rove wrote a column saying, "not that facts matter much to The Donald." Tweet, July 16, 2015.

@FrankLuntz is a low class slob who came to my office looking for consulting work and I had zero interest. Now he picks anti-Trump panels!

> *Frank Luntz conducts focus groups for Fox during GOP debates. Tweet, August 7, 2015.*

Why does @FoxNews keep George Will as a talking head? Wrong on so many subjects!

> *On August 12, George Will wrote that Trump is a "counterfeit Republican." Tweet, August 17, 2015.*

Do you believe that highly overrated political pundit @krauthammer said this is the best Republican field in 35 years. What a dope!

On July 8, Charles Krauthammer, a Fox News commentator, said talking about Trump "is a complete waste of time." Tweet, July 9, 2015.

Thank you @krauthammer for your nice comments on @oreillyfactor. A lot of progress is being made!

Tweet, August 3, 2015.

The hatred that clown @krauthammer has for me is unbelievable—causes him to lie when many others say Trump easily won debate.

Earlier in the day, Krauthammer said on Fox that Trump's performance at the GOP presidential debate the night before showed "the collapse of Trump." Tweet, August 7, 2015.

@TheJuanWilliams you never speak well of me & yet when I saw you at Fox you ran over like a child and wanted a picture.

On June 16, Juan Williams said Trump's ego is "just on fire." Tweet, July 3, 2015.

Roger Ailes just called. He is a great guy & assures me that "Trump" will be treated fairly on @FoxNews. His word is always good!

Tweet, August 10, 2015.

DEBATE ANALYSIS

The fact is, [the debates are] all about ratings, whether we like it or not.

Interviewed by Colin Cowherd on The Herd, *Fox Sports One, November 2, 2015.*

I've led every debate, number one in every debate, which you know, and I couldn't say it unless I did.

Interviewed by Sean Hannity on Hannity, *Fox News, November 3, 2015.*

It was the largest broadcast in the history of CNN. Think of it. With all the wars, this was number one. I wonder how many people would have been watching if I wasn't there. Three?

Speech at South Carolina African American Chamber of Commerce, North Charleston, South Carolina, September 23, 2015.

My moral authority is better than his moral authority, that I can tell you.

> *Comparing himself to CNBC's John Harwood,*
> *who raised the issue of Trump's moral authority.*
> *Interviewed by Bill O'Reilly on* The O'Reilly
> Factor, *Fox News, October 29, 2015.*

9/11: FALLEN HEROES (AND OTHER MATTERS)

Let's all take a moment to remember all of the heroes from a very tragic day that we cannot let happen again!

Tweet, September 11, 2015, at 11:19 a.m.

Just purchased NBC's half of The Miss Universe Organization and settled all lawsuits against them. Now own 100%—stay tuned!

Tweet, September 11, 2015, at 11:31 a.m.

TRUMPLANDIA

★　　★　　★

I will absolutely apologize
sometime hopefully in the distant
future if I'm ever wrong.

BOOTSTRAPS

It has not been easy for me. It has not been
easy for me. And, you know, I started off in
Brooklyn. My father gave me a small loan of a
million dollars.

Interviewed by Matt Lauer on The Today Show,
NBC, Atkinson, New Hampshire, October 26, 2015.

I felt that I was in the military in the true
sense because I dealt with the people.

Never Enough: Donald Trump and the
Pursuit of Success, *Michael D'Antonio (New
York: Thomas Dunne Books, 2015), 70.*

NO APOLOGIES

Apologizing's a great thing but you have to be wrong. I will absolutely apologize sometime hopefully in the distant future if I'm ever wrong.

Interviewed by Jimmy Fallon on The Tonight Show With Jimmy Fallon, *NBC, September 11, 2015.*

I apologize when I'm wrong. ... I said nothing wrong.

Refusing to apologize for his comments about Megyn Kelly. Interviewed by Chuck Todd, Meet the Press, *NBC, August 9, 2015.*

When will people, and the media, start to apologize to me for my statement, "Mexico is sending….", which turned out to be true?

Tweet, July 13, 2015.

(See Give Me Your Tired, Your Poor, page 84)

I won't do that, because I've said nothing wrong.

Refusing to apologize to Jeb Bush's wife after saying Bush's immigration policy was influenced by the fact that his wife was born in Mexico. GOP presidential debate, September 16, 2015.

I would never say bad about any religion.
I didn't say anything bad about it. I would
certainly give an apology if I said something
bad about it.

Earlier, Trump said he is a Presbyterian but
he didn't know about Seventh-day Adventists.
Dr. Ben Carson is a Seventh-day Adventist.
Interviewed by George Stephanopoulos on
This Week, *ABC News, October 25, 2015.*

(See page 20)

The young intern who accidentally did a
Retweet apologizes.

Responding to his retweet of a suggestion that
Dr. Ben Carson's lead in the Iowa polls could be
due to "too much Monsanto in the corn [creating]
issues in the brain." Tweet, October 22, 2015.

APOLOGIES

THE ART OF WAR

On July 1, 2015, Macy's announced it would no longer carry Donald Trump's ties and men's fragrance, called Success by Trump, following his remarks about Mexican immigrants, who he said were rapists and drug dealers. This, after Macy's received a petition from over 700,000 people calling on the store to drop Trump products.

For all of those who want to #MakeAmericaGreatAgain, boycott @Macys. They are weak on border security & stopping illegal immigration.

Tweet, July 1, 2015.

So many people calling to say they are cutting up their @Macys credit card. Thank you!

Tweet, July 2, 2015.

Boycott @Macys… MAKE AMERICA GREAT AGAIN!

Tweet, July 11, 2015.

I hope the boycott of @Macys continues forever. So many people are cutting up their cards. Macy's stores suck and they are bad for U.S.A.

Tweet, July 16, 2015.

Wow, @Macys shares are down more than 40% this year. I never knew my ties & shirts not being sold there would have such a big impact!

Tweet, November 16, 2015.

TRUTHINESS

I never said that. I never said that.

Denying he disparaged Senator Marco Rubio by claiming Rubio was Mark Zuckerberg's "personal senator" for wanting to increase visas for skilled workers. (The information appeared on Trump's presidential website.) GOP presidential debate, October 28, 2015.

Our president wants to take in 250,000 [immigrants] from Syria.

Repeating a false claim from a fake news story, which quotes State Department spokeswoman Cathy Pieper. There is no State Department spokeswoman by that name. Speech in Beaumont, Texas, November 13, 2015.

I predicted Osama bin Laden. In my book, I predicted terrorism. Because I can feel it, like I feel a good location, OK?

Trump's book refers to news accounts which he said described Bin Laden as "public enemy number one." Nashville, Tennessee, November 16, 2015.

So if you're a [Syrian] Christian, you can't get into the United States. If you're a Muslim, it's one of the easiest ways to get into the United States from Syria.

Hannity, *November 17, 2015.*

I watched in Jersey City, NJ, where thousands and thousands of people were cheering as that building was coming down. Thousands of people were cheering.

Trump describing what he said he saw on 9/11. (In an interview with George Stephanopoulos, Trump said he saw it on TV.) Birmingham, Alabama, November 21, 2015.

I think Ronald Reagan liked me a lot more than he liked a lot of other people.

Speech at South Carolina African American Chamber of Commerce, North Charleston, South Carolina, September 23, 2015.

(For more on Truthiness, read the rest of the book.)

HUMILITY

Humble.

Answering a question about what his Secret Service
code name would be if he were elected president.
GOP presidential debate, September 16, 2015.

HIS CROWNING GLORY

I don't wear a toupée. It's my hair.

Rally in Greenville, South Carolina, August 27, 2015.

Number one is my hair… It may not be pretty, but it's mine.

Answering a question about the biggest misconception about him. Interviewed by Carson Daly on The Today Show, *NBC, Atkinson, New Hampshire, October 26, 2015.*

Real quick, we don't want to mess it up too much because I do use hair spray.

Asking a female member of the audience to come on stage to feel his hair to prove it's not a toupée. Speech in Greenville, South Carolina, August 27, 2015.

★

I HAVE BETTER HAIR THAN HE DOES, RIGHT?

★

COMPARING HIS MANE TO MARCO RUBIO'S.
SPEECH AT SOUTH CAROLINA AFRICAN AMERICAN
CHAMBER OF COMMERCE, NORTH CHARLESTON,
SOUTH CAROLINA, SEPTEMBER 23, 2015.

LICENSE TO CARRY

I'm very strong in favor of the Second Amendment. … I have a license to carry.

Interviewed by Bill O'Reilly on The O'Reilly Factor, *Fox News, October 29, 2015.*

You know, the president is thinking about signing an executive order where he wants to take your guns away. You hear about this? Not gonna happen. That won't happen. But that's a tough one, I think that's a tough one for him to do. There's plenty of executive orders being signed, you know that. And we can't let that go on.

Speech in Anderson, South Carolina, October 19, 2015.

No, no. I've heard that he wants to. And I heard it, I think, on your network. Somebody said that that's what he's thinking about. I didn't say that he's signing it. I said I think that would be a tough one to sign, actually.

Pulling back from his claim that President Obama was thinking about repealing the Second Amendment. Interviewed by Alisyn Camerota on New Day, *CNN, October 20, 2015.*

Say what you want, but if they had guns… if they were allowed to carry—it would have been a much, much different situation.

Commenting on the mass killings by ISIS in Paris the day before. Speech in Beaumont, Texas, November 14, 2015.

You're going to have these things happen and it's a horrible thing to behold, horrible.

Replying to a question about how a President Trump would deal with mass shootings. Interviewed by Willie Geist on Morning Joe, *MSNBC, October 2, 2015.*

My warmest condolences to the families of the horrible Roseburg, Oregon, shootings.

Responding to the killing of nine people at Umpqua Community College in Oregon. Tweet, October 1, 2015.

GAY MARRIAGE

I'm for traditional marriage.

> *Trump is on his third traditional marriage.*
> *Conservative Political Action Conference*
> *(CPAC), February 27, 2015.*

SATURDAY NIGHT FUN

Hosting it's a bigger deal than doing the single skit.

> *Comparing his hosting of* Saturday Night Live *to when Hillary Clinton appeared in one of the show's skits several weeks earlier. Interviewed by Chuck Todd,* Meet the Press, *NBC, November 8, 2015.*

(See Hillary Clinton, page 71)

I know these groups; many of them are scam groups.

Talking about organizations that protested his hosting Saturday Night Live, *such as the League of United Latin American Citizens (LULAC), the Hispanic Federation, the Labor Council for Latin American Advancement (LCLAA), the National Hispanic Media Coalition, and other organizations. Interviewed by Alisyn Camerota on* New Day, CNN, *October 20, 2015.*

It was funny and the place was roaring. I can tell you the studio, inside the studio, they were roaring.

Saying Larry David's scripted line on SNL, "*Trump's a racist," was said all in good fun. Interviewed by Chuck Todd,* Meet the Press, NBC, *November 8, 2015.*

CHALLENGES OF
THE COMPUTER AGE

I'm not a big fan of the email stuff.

Interviewed by Hugh Hewitt on The Hugh Hewitt
Show, *Salem Radio Network, October 22, 2015.*

In the old days when you wanted to attack you had a courier with armed guards and you'd have an envelope and you'd give it to the general. Now you send it to the general and you have no idea how many people are watching and reading. They're hacking your messages. I think [General] MacArthur would not like the whole concept of computers.

Interviewed by Hugh Hewitt on The Hugh Hewitt Show, *Salem Radio Network, October 22, 2015.*

FAMILY VALUES

Yeah, she's really something, and what a beauty, that one. If I weren't happily married and, you know, her *father*...

> *Referring to his daughter, Ivanka Trump, executive vice president of development and acquisitions, the Trump Organization. "Trump Seriously: On the Trail With the GOP's Tough Guy," Paul Solotaroff,* Rolling Stone, *September 9, 2015.*

My wife said, "You know if you run you know you're going to win." She's actually very smart.

> *Speech at South Carolina African American Chamber of Commerce, North Charleston, South Carolina, September 23, 2015.*

BEWARE

I will see what happens. I have to be treated fairly.

> *Trump, who signed a pledge two months earlier*
> *to support the GOP nominee, discussing whether*
> *he'd consider becoming a third party candidate.*
> ABC This Week, *November 22, 2015.*

PRESIDENT
TRUMP

★ ★ ★

I want my generals kicking ass.

BOMB THE SHIT
OUT OF THEM

I would say I'm the most militaristic person on the stage.

Interviewed by Joe Scarborough on Morning Joe, *MSNBC, November 11, 2015.*

When you talk about the nuclear button, the ones I'm worried about are the other people on the other side that have the nuclear. But don't worry about me...

Responding to Sean Hannity's question, "You'll have your finger on the button. Are you ready for the onslaught, the avalanche, if you will, of criticisms that will come your way?" Interviewed by Sean Hannity on Hannity, *Fox News, June 17, 2015.*

I would bomb the shit out of them.

Describing his strategy for fighting
Islamic terrorists. Speech in Fort
Dodge, Iowa, November 12, 2015.

I know more about ISIS than the generals do.

Speech in Fort Dodge, Iowa, November 12, 2015.

You bomb the hell out of the oil. Don't worry about the cities. The cities are terrible.

Responding to a question about Syria and the
Middle East. Interviewed by Sean Hannity
on Hannity, Fox News, June 17, 2015.

You kill them at the head.

Responding to a question about ISIS and the Middle East. Interviewed by Sean Hannity on Hannity, *Fox News, June 17, 2015.*

I'm not looking to quagmire...

Interviewed by George Stephanopoulos on This Week, *ABC News, November 8, 2015.*

I want my generals kicking ass.

Speech in Burlington, Iowa, October 21, 2015.

If you think of General MacArthur and General Patton, these people don't talk on television about what they're doing with battles and everything else.

Interviewed by Matt Lauer and Willie Geist on The Today Show, *NBC, Atkinson, New Hampshire, October 26, 2015.*

I am the toughest guy. I will rebuild our military... Nobody's going to mess with us.

Trump's next line was drowned out with audience chants of "USA! USA! USA!" Rally in Mobile, Alabama, August 21, 2015.

DISRESPECTED

We're being laughed at all over the world.

Conservative Political Action Conference
(CPAC), February 27, 2015.

When was the last time anybody saw us
beating, let's say, China, in a trade deal? They
kill us. I beat China all the time. All the time.

Announcing his run for president, Trump
Tower, New York City, June 16, 2015.

What China did to us is the single greatest theft, it's the single greatest robbery in the history of the world. It's true. ... China rebuilt China with our money. And I love China. They buy my apartments. They're great. They're getting away with murder, they know it. I get along with them fine—they're tenants of mine in buildings. They're great.

Rally in Jacksonville, Florida, October 24, 2015.

We are a whipping post. We are a laughingstock as a country. We're not respected anymore. And that's why I decided to run for president.

Interviewed by Sean Hannity on Hannity, Fox News, June 17, 2015.

[ISIS has] better access to Internet than we do. I mean, they're recruiting people from our country and who knows what they're planning?

Interviewed by George Stephanopoulos on
This Week, ABC News, November 8, 2015.

China is a bully to us...

Interviewed by Sean Hannity on
Hannity, Fox News, June 17, 2015.

Mexico is ripping off the United States big league.

Conservative Political Action Conference
(CPAC), February 27, 2015.

No, not a comic book, and it's not a very nicely asked question the way you say that.

Answering John Harwood's question, "Is this a
comic book version of a presidential campaign?"
GOP presidential debate, October 28, 2015.

BRING THAT
SUCKER BACK

The #IranDeal is a catastrophe that must
be stopped. Will lead to at least partial world
destruction & make Iran a force like never
before.

Tweet, August 11, 2015.

#IranDeal will go down as one of the dumbest
& most dangerous misjudgments ever entered
into in history of our country—incompetent
leader!

Tweet, July 28, 2015.

[The deal was] done by incompetent people
and they should be ashamed of themselves.

Iowa Faith & Freedom Coalition Presidential
Forum, Des Moines, Iowa, September 19, 2015.

Even when you have incompetents like
Obama and Kerry, there's always something
in a contract that you can hang your hat on.
That's what I do. There's always something.
I will find it and, believe me, I will bring that
sucker back.

Rally in Jacksonville, Florida, October 24, 2015.

I will stop Iran from getting nuclear weapons. And we won't be using a man like Secretary Kerry that has absolutely no concept of negotiation, who's making a horrible and laughable deal, who's just being tapped along as they make weapons right now, and then goes into a bicycle race at seventy-two years old and falls and breaks his leg. I won't be doing that. And I promise I will never be in a bicycle race. That I can tell you.

Announcing his run for president, Trump Tower, New York City, June 16, 2015.

STANDING UP
TO PUTIN

Well, first of all, it's not only Russia. We have problems with North Korea where they actually have nuclear weapons, you know, nobody talks about it. We talk about Iran, and that's one of the worst deals ever made. One of the worst contracts ever signed, ever, in anything, and it's a disgrace. But, we have somebody over there, a madman, who already has nuclear weapons. We don't talk about that. That's a problem. China is a problem, both economically in what they're doing in the South China Sea, I mean, they are becoming a very, very major force. So, we have more than just Russia. But, as far as the

Ukraine is concerned, and you could Syria—
as far as Syria, I like—if Putin wants to go
in, and I got to know him very well because
we were both on 60 Minutes, we were stable
mates, and we did very well that night. But,
you know that. But, if Putin wants to go and
knock the hell out of ISIS, I am all for it, 100
percent and I can't understand how anybody
would be against it...

*Responding to the succinct question, "What
does President Trump do in response to
Russia's aggression?" GOP presidential
debate, November 10, 2015.*

I will get along—I think—with Putin, and I will get along with others, and we will have a much more stable, stable world.

GOP presidential debate, September 16, 2015.

We need some unpredictability. We really do. ... We're so predictable. ... We're playing against Putin.

Speech in Greenville, South Carolina, August 27, 2015.

NOT GOING TO HAPPEN

The problem we have right now—we have a society that sits back and says we're not going to do anything. And eventually the 50 percent cannot carry, and it's unfair to them, but cannot carry the other 50 percent.

Interviewed by Sean Hannity on Hannity, Fox News, June 17, 2015.

We have a disaster called the big lie: Obamacare.

Announcing his run for president, Trump Tower, New York City, June 16, 2015.

Obamacare really kicks in in '16, 2016. Obama is going to be out playing golf. He might be on one of my courses. I would invite him, I actually would say. I have the best courses in the world… I have one right next to the White House, right on the Potomac. If he'd like to play, that's fine.

Announcing his run for president, Trump Tower, New York City, June 16, 2015.

Look at the Department of Education… They're telling people from Iowa and other places and New Hampshire how to educate your children. There's so much waste and we have to stop this.

Zeroing in on the early caucus and primary states. Interviewed by Sean Hannity on Hannity, Fox News, June 17, 2015.

A man came up to me yesterday and said, "You know, Mr. Trump, I've been coming to this place [the Trump National Doral in Florida] for twenty-five years. If you can do the same job for the United States of America as you did making this place incredible"—because it's the best resort in the country now—he said, "Wow, would that be something!" I said, "That's what I'm going to do!"

Rally in Jacksonville, Florida, October 24, 2015.

Washington (D.C.) is such a mess— nothing works! I will MAKE AMERICA GREAT AGAIN! It's not going to happen with anyone else.

Tweet, October 8, 2015.

THE RETURN OF RUDOLPH

If I become president, we're all going to be saying "Merry Christmas" again, that I can tell you.

Speech in Springfield, Illinois, November 9, 2015.

I'm a good Christian. If I become president, we're gonna be saying "Merry Christmas" at every store... You can leave "happy holidays" at the corner.

Speech in Burlington, Iowa, October 21, 2015.

You go to a store in New York City, they don't have Christmas anymore. They don't put it up. They don't use the word. You take your boy to Macy's, you take your boy to these stores, they don't have the word. I want people to be able to celebrate Christmas. All right? Somebody said, 'That's not the biggest part.' I said, 'It's a big part, a big part.' You know what they're doing? Every year it gets worse and worse. Before you know it, you won't be able to go to church the way they're doing it.

Iowa Faith & Freedom Coalition Presidential Forum, Des Moines, Iowa, September 19, 2015.

Maybe we should boycott Starbucks.

Reacting to a decision by Starbucks to serve coffee in red cups, sans Santa and snowmen, during the 2015 holiday season. Speech in Springfield, Illinois, November 9, 2015.

THE BEST &
THE BRIGHTEST

Thank you Sarah—Let's have pizza in New
York soon with you & your great family

> *Responding to a Facebook post by Sarah*
> *Palin saying, "Mr. Trump should know he's*
> *doing something right when the malcontents*
> *go ballistic..." Tweet, June 17, 2015.*

I like Sarah Palin a lot. I think Sarah Palin has got the very unfair press. I think the press has treated her very unfairly. But I would pick somebody that would be a terrific—you know, you have to view it as really who would be a good president in case something happened. But I would—there are many, many people out there that I think would be very good.

Sort of answering a question about whether he would pick Sarah Palin as his running mate. Interviewed by Jonathan Karl on This Week, *ABC News, August 2, 2015.*

Listening to @rushlimbaugh on way back to Jury Duty. Fantastic show, terrific guy!

Tweet, August 17, 2015.

Thank you @AnnCoulter for your nice words. The U.S. is becoming a dumping ground for the world. Pols don't get it. Make America Great Again!

In an earlier conversation with Bill Maher, Ann Coulter had said that, of the announced candidates, Trump offered the best chance for Republicans to win back the White House. Tweet, June 20, 2015.

Highly respected economist @Larry_Kudlow
is a big fan of my tax plan—thank you Larry.

Tweet, September 30, 2015.

Happy Birthday to the great @BillyGraham.
He's done so many wonderful things, not the
least of which is his fantastic family. I love
Billy!

Tweet, November 6, 2015.

THE UNIFIER

I have a great temperament. My temperament
is very good, very calm.

GOP presidential debate, September 16, 2015.

I'm a counterpuncher. I can't hit people who
don't hit me. Maybe that's my weakness.

"Introducing Donald Trump, Diplomat,"
Maureen Dowd, The New York
Times, *August 15, 2015.*

I really am a nice person. I give tremendous amounts of money away. I love people...

Answering a question about whether he's too harsh to be president. Interviewed by Willie Geist on The Today Show, *NBC, Atkinson, New Hampshire, October 26, 2015.*

People are tired of nice.

Interviewed by Willie Geist on The Today Show, *NBC, Atkinson, New Hampshire, October 26, 2015.*

I get along with everybody. ... I'll be the greatest unifier of all.

Speech in Sioux City, Iowa, October 27, 2015.

ON DAY ONE

First thing I'd do on my first day as president is close up our borders so that illegal immigrants cannot come into our country.

Twitter Q&A, September 21, 2015.

If I get elected, first day they're gone. Gangs all over the place. Chicago, Baltimore, no matter where you look.

GOP presidential debate, September 16, 2015.

★

I KNOW HOW TO DO IT. I REALLY KNOW HOW TO DO IT.

★

AFTER A NINETY-FIVE-MINUTE RANT, TELLING THE AUDIENCE HE KNOWS HOW TO BE PRESIDENT. SPEECH IN FORT DODGE, IOWA, NOVEMBER 12, 2015.

THE AMERICAN DREAM

We're going to make our country great again.
Remember this: the American dream will be
back, bigger and stronger, I promise, than
ever before. Ever.

Rally in Jacksonville, Florida, October 24, 2015.

Remember, official campaign merchandise
(hats, apparel etc.) can only be bought at
donaldjtrump.com. Be careful, don't get
ripped-off

Tweet, October 23, 2015.

ACKNOWLEDGMENTS

He wasn't going to be my husband's favorite houseguest, that I knew. But once I started, the rest was inevitable. At breakfast, in the evening by the fire, and in the middle of the night, I'd spout quotes from the day's haul of Trumpedia. My husband, Dan Detzner, tolerated my latest obsession, knowing we'd soon return to our regularly scheduled program—well, until I'd find another bright idea. Dan, a professor of American Studies at the University of Minnesota, coined my favorite term: Trumplandia.

Having a loving partner makes everything better.

Dan and my sister, Susan Pogash, edited the manuscript, immensely improving it. Thank you, Susan, for being my best friend, ally, and marketer, and for always looking out for your little sis.

My daughter, Rachel Wood, fielded emergency tech support calls, emails, and text messages on nights and weekends. Calmly (unlike her mother), she walked me through every crisis, which is more than I can say for Comcast, whose service was reliably intermittent. And, child, I hope you're kidding when below your name you wrote:

Tech Support (Ret.)

Thank you to my drummer son, Jake Wood, for your rock-out music. As an antidote to life in Trumplandia, I found daily release by dancing and hiking to Diego's Umbrella, Jake's great gypsy rock band.

I appreciate the love and support of my

son John Wood and of the rest my family and friends.

My late husband, Jim Wood, proved a person could be both erudite and outrageously funny. And he believed in me.

The idea for this book popped into my head in early summer of 2015. Each time Donald Trump uttered another shocking statement, he reinforced my belief that somebody had to collect his words, discover the patterns, and tell his stories.

Thank you, Jon Stewart, Stephen Colbert, and your writers, for showing me the way.

My longtime agent, Sterling Lord, instantly got the concept of *Quotations* and raced to find a great publisher. There aren't many publishing houses that operate at such a high level and as fast as newspaper reporters; everyone at RosettaBooks does. They have been a joy to work with. Thank you to Arthur Klebanoff for supporting the book and to Jay McNair who made major cuts that were so good, I didn't bleed. The cover design by Corina Lupp raised my spirits and spurred me on. I appreciate Hannah Bennett's deadline edits and the meticulous fact checking of Sara Brady.

It wasn't easy having them as parents, but Israel and Sylvia Pogash taught me to be engaged.

My father emigrated from Russia when he was a small boy. He was a left-wing skeptic and a witty cynic, but for the rest of his long life he remained grateful to this country for taking him in. While there were times he worried about shifting political moods, he had an abiding faith that in the end the American people would do the right thing.

ABOUT THE EDITOR

Carol Pogash is an all-terrain writer. She's been a newspaper reporter and columnist, magazine writer and editor, TV reporter, internet editor and writer, radio essayist and author. In recent years most of her articles have been published in *The New York Times* on the front page and in National, Arts & Leisure, Business, Science, Style, Sports and Op Ed sections.

She's covered AIDS, homelessness, a Golden Gate Bridge suicide barrier, and the country's first cat café.

Pogash is the author of two previous books: *As Real As It Gets: The Life of a Hospital at the Center of the AIDS Epidemic*, with a foreword by Randy Shilts, and *Seduced by Madness: The True Story of the Susan Polk Murder Case*. Pogash tweets at @cpogash.